The New SPELL-WELL

Book 6

C J Ridout

BLACKIE

Contents

PAGE

How to be a good speller — 4
Guidelines for writing — 5
Spelling groups are on all left-hand pages — 6–26
Terror—twenty fathoms deep! — 7
Wintry weather — 9
A holiday abroad — 11
The year is 2050 — 13
The day I met the Queen — 15
A tale of the supernatural — 17
An eye-witness account of a sporting event — 19
Raising funds for charity — 21
A day in the life of a policeman — 23
A walking or cycling holiday — 25
The day I was accused of shoplifting — 27
Words with similar meaning — 28 – 46
Concise descriptions — 29
Mood — 31
The season I like best — 33
Road safety — 35
My favourite hobby — 37
Discussion — 39
Personal letters — 41
Addressing envelopes — 43
Conversations — 45
Writing a play — 47
Business letters — 48
Posters — 50
Roots, prefixes, suffixes — 52
Difficult words — 53–5
Do you know where these sayings came from? — 56
Abbreviations — 58
About parliament — 59
About cathedrals and churches, About the theatre — 60
About meetings, About shops — 62
Proverbs or sayings — 63

BLACKIE & SON LTD.
Bishopbriggs, Glasgow G64 2NZ
7 Leicester Place,
London WC2H 7BP

ISBN 0 216 90618 0

Printed in Great Britain by
G.N.P.-Booth Ltd. Glasgow

How to be a good speller

1 Look at each word knowing that you will have to write it later without help.

2 Say each word clearly and pronounce it correctly. Sometimes we are careless in the way we say words and this makes spelling more difficult.

3 Be clear about the meaning or meanings of each word so that you can use it to make an interesting sentence.

4 As you say the word look at each part so that you know the difficulties.

5 Close your eyes and trace the word with your finger. Check that you traced it correctly then do it a few more times so that you will *never* forget.

6 Keep an alphabetically arranged word book and *neatly* note down all the words you have learned.

7 Learn the words *you* use! When writing a story, use your dictionary to help you spell words you do not know. Learn these words in the same way as you learn the words in this book. Remember to add these words to your word book! *A good speller is someone who knows how to spell the words he uses in his writing.*

Guidelines for writing

When writing a composition you must plan how you will present your work. The following approach will help you.

Think of all the ideas you can about the subject. Now plan:

A beginning: How you will provide a background for your story. You must set the scene and arouse the interest and curiosity of your reader.

A middle: How the main points in the story will be arranged so that they are presented in proper order. Consider how you will bring the story to life for your reader. You may do this by thoughtful description. Think of things you would:

      see   hear   touch   smell

Describe these in such a way that your reader can share your experiences.

Try to make your reader feel the things you feel.

Try to strike the right mood so that your reader feels that he is involved.

An end: How you will round off the story and maintain interest to the last sentence.

Think of different ways you can present your work. For example you may choose to write:

a story   a description   a poem
a letter   a report   a play

Sometimes it is interesting to write about the same topic in different ways.

1	2	3
coffee	thieves	horizon
decree	grieve	melon
degree	reprieve	salmon
trustee	tier	octagon
pedigree	wield	abandon

4	5	6
awry	altar	dismal
wrestle	mortar	normal
wristlet	cedar	vital
wrapper	briar	mortal
wrongful	burglar	sandals

7	8	9
surprise	syrup	spectre
survive	syringe	fibre
surpass	system	theatre
surmount	sylvan	sombre
surname	myth	calibre

10	11	12
*translate	taught	**icy
transform	taut	bony
transgress	taunt	stony
transpire	gaudy	healthy
transit	gauze	guilty

* Latin prefix *trans-* = across, beyond
** Suffix *-y* = having the nature of

Terror—twenty fathoms deep!

yacht
channel
ocean
current
torrent
grotto
cavern
sea-bed
outcrop
fissure
catastrophe
shipwreck
valve
air-lock
cylinder
oxygen
life-line
obstacle
fatigue
strength
coral
fronds
barnacles
squid
tentacles

tranquil
pressurized
gloomy
luminous
translucent
limpid
treacherous
defective
faulty
jagged
immense
hideous
grotesque
malevolent
serrated
encrusted
engulfed
buried
voracious
undulating
weird
vulnerable
timely
unconscious
suffocating

encounter
sustain
manoeuvre
manipulate
distinguish
endure
enthrall
fascinate
overshadow
smother
choke
breathe
inhale
gape
glimmer
skulk
writhe
wrench
heave
veer
threaten
terrorize
subdue
squirm
impale

Phrases

a strong undertow
panic-stricken
submerged relics

an alien world
timeless drift
green gloom

1	2	3
severe	violet	century
revere	pious	census
cohere	cider	censure
adhere	client	censor
sincere	siren	celery

4	5	6
Egypt	civil	admit
accept	peril	emit
except	perilous	stitches
exempt	fulfil	witness
contempt	distil	summit

7	8	9
volley	circuit	safeguard
valley	circular	guildhall
pulley	circulation	guessing
motto	circumference	rogue
Scottish	circumstance	roguery

10	11	12
*departure	strew	**primrose
deported	strewn	primitive
depress	shrewd	primate
defend	pew	primary
descend	sinew	primeval

* Latin prefix *de-* = down, from, away
** Latin root *primus* = first

Wintry weather

landscape
valley
vegetation
desolation
forecast
temperature
cloudburst
drizzle
thermometer
barometer
depression
horizon
outline
silhouette
seed-capsules
hedgerows
prospect
hardship
autumn
quagmire
traveller
pheasant
squirrel

overcast
sombre
dismal
forlorn
arctic
seasonal
predominant
muffled
neglected
dulling
voracious
unpleasant
melancholy
biting
dank
bleak
moist
flooded
panoramic
overgrown
entangled
rotting
moaning

hibernate
venture
yearn
saturate
loom
freeze
huddle
recall
envelop
scud
brood
disappear
cascade
penetrate
obscure
obliterate
reflect
descend

hopefully
relentlessly
partially
mercilessly

Phrases

shafts of sunlight
nature's transformation
tell-tale footprints
frosted window panes
snow-capped mountains

windswept heath
numbed fingers
impenetrable mist
swollen torrent
crashing waves

1	2	3
baggage	meant	tonic
passage	threaten	tropics
pilgrimage	increase	politics
beverage	earnest	Pacific
courage	yearn	tactics

4	5	6
goddess	stile	enemy's
gossip	reptile	everybody's
possibly	docile	lady's
tennis	reconcile	ladies'
trellis	defile	thrush's

7	8	9
type	weird	succeed
typical	seized	veneer
thyme	deceive	volunteer
cyclone	receive	mountaineer
asylum	receipt	engineer

10	11	12
*exclaim	debt	**conserve
exhale	doubt	preserve
excavate	numb	preservative
exhaust	plumber	reserve
exterior	succumb	reservoir

* Latin prefix *ex-* = out, out of, beyond
** Latin root *servo* = I keep

A holiday abroad

Channel
hovercraft
ferry
tunnel
aeroplane
timetable
schedule
programme
ticket
passport
currency
luggage
berth
quay
cafeteria
restaurant
chateau
chalet
frontier
official
tariff
vineyard
courier

souvenir
memento
glacier
region
temperature
climate
language

continental
picturesque
historic
ancient
principal
sun-drenched
foreign
European
national
dissimilar
plentiful
unforgettable
memorable
indispensable
essential

embark
disembark
exchange
purchase
translate
sightsee
sunbathe
communicate
savour
sample
taste
roam
comprehend
embarrass
converse
consult
pronounce
declare

typically
cautiously
daily
tentatively

Phrases

bon voyage
immigration control
duty-free perfume
local specialities
multi-lingual shopkeepers

a rough crossing
customs officers
pavement cafés
an interesting excursion
adjust your watches

1	2	3
currant	dodge	engine
radiant	wedge	genuine
vagrant	cartridge	gesture
abundant	partridge	genius
defendant	drudgery	gypsy

4	5	6
gallop	pounce	guide
gallant	renounce	guidance
satellite	pronounce	guest
channel	announce	guilt
tunnel	announcement	guile

7	8	9
orphan	instance	creature
sulphur	penance	posture
sphere	attendance	fracture
phantom	abundance	conjure
pamphlet	endurance	azure

10	11	12
*export	**useful	**plentiful
deport	thoughtful	bountiful
report	powerful	merciful
transport	grateful	dutiful
porter	successful	beautiful

* Latin root *porto* = I carry
** Suffix -*ful* = having much of, full of

The year is 2050

progress
leisure
conservation
pollution
agriculture
architecture
civilization
culture
environment
surroundings
dwellings
design
furnishings
fashion
transport
recreation
entertainment
pastime
relaxation
resources
automata
experience
disease
landscape

modern
current
beneficial
ingenious
incredible
far-reaching
feasible
extraordinary
exotic
inconceivable
unimaginable
unbelievable
durable
permanent
infinite
immense
marvellous
celestial
outmoded
obsolete
old-fashioned
familiar
peculiar
harmonious

forecast
prophesy
predict
invent
manufacture
prosper
evolve
accomplish
acquire
encapsulate
recycle
energize
flourish
mechanize
endeavour
baffle
contemplate
excite
explore
orbit
commemorate
preserve
commute
inhabit

Phrases

intergalactic travel
a recent discovery
frontiers of knowledge
an obliging robot

science fiction
a brief sojourn
the latest craze
fruitful deserts

1	2	3
abrupt	scaffold	lessen
corrupt	scorched	essence
corruption	scarcely	essential
captive	scheme	residence
capture	sceptic	residential

4	5	6
hygiene	judge	cede
hyacinth	lodge	recede
hymn	judgment	concede
hydrogen	knowledge	intercede
hyena	abridge	accede

7	8	9
realm	possess	vinegar
dearth	mattress	boundary
rehearse	gossip	dictionary
rehearsal	cypress	February
headquarters	empress	Spaniard

10	11	12
*portable	infection	**marine
eatable	erected	mariner
enjoyable	reflect	maritime
comfortable	project	submarine
noticeable	rectangle	mermaid

* Suffix -able = capable of being, able to
** Latin root mare = sea

The day I met the Queen

sovereign
escort
prince
princess
entourage
limousine
retinue
procession
dignitary
representatives
reception
interview
speech
photographer
conversation
address
decoration
medal
cavalcade
spectators
enthusiasm
itinerary
barrier

appearance
orchestra
invitation
dais
ceremony
bodyguard

solemn
dignified
distinguished
memorable
majestic
royal
elegant
immaculate
courteous
gracious
unforgettable
jubilant
spectacular
enthusiastic
patriotic
overawed

compliment
honour
attend
applaud
present
congratulate
decorate
adorn
advance
curtsy
retire
circulate
converse
acclaim
pose

politely
respectfully
enthusiastically
nervously
gracefully
deferentially
proudly

Phrases

guard of honour
bouquet of flowers
lined the route
stood to attention
an historic occasion

ladies-in-waiting
National Anthem
an official opening
Duke of Edinburgh Award
an unscheduled stop

1	2	3
delude	commotion	auction
latitude	commander	auctioneer
platitude	commandeer	hauled
longitude	comment	launched
altitude	commit	assault

4	5	6
factor	rebel	partial
factory	rebellion	martial
satisfactory	compel	initial
editor	compelling	artificial
protector	repelled	parochial

7	8	9
dignity	licence	separate
indignity	silence	intricate
indignant	commence	legitimate
dignified	commencement	appropriate
indignation	tendency	ultimate

10	11	12
*prefix	scythe	**visible
predict	sceptre	edible
prefect	scissors	credible
prefer	scenery	legible
precaution	science	flexible

* Latin prefix *pre-* = before
** Suffix *-ible* = that can be

A tale of the supernatural

ghoul
spectre
presence
demon
poltergeist
silhouette
apparition
skeleton
occasion
shriek
phantom
visitation
graveyard
cemetery
rumour
gossip
confusion
legend
suicide
victim
experience
assassin
vengeance

haunted
bewitched
ghoulish
invisible
noisy
shadowy
vague
existence
mysterious
malevolent
gruesome
weird
creaking
rattling
petrified
grating
hypnotic
illusive
lamenting
wailing
fleeting
eerie
headless

dilapidated
notorious
infamous
dreadful

materialize
mesmerize
glide
interrupt
approach
horrify
escape
flee
recollect
imagine
challenge
wager
exaggerate
disbelieve
hesitate
terrorize

simultaneously

Phrases

echoing footsteps
hollow laughter
a sudden chill
tingle of apprehension
cold light of day

blood-curdling scream
as midnight struck
flickering firelight
icy fingers
a knowing look

1	2	3
decimal	massive	fiction
chemical	massacre	elocution
poetical	assassin	sanction
cannibal	harass	ambition
prodigal	carcass	exception

4	5	6
issue	ignore	extinct
revenue	ignorant	instinct
avenue	ignite	distinct
retinue	ignition	indistinct
tissue	ignoble	succinct

7	8	9
chemistry	pavilion	indicate
choral	criterion	indication
chorister	million	vocation
architect	vermillion	dislocation
character	dominion	lubrication

10	11	12
*postpone	impel	**interval
postscript	impelled	interfere
post-mortem	repel	international
post-war	repellent	interpret
posthumous	dispel	intervene

* Latin prefix *post-* = after
** Latin prefix *inter-* = between

An eye-witness account of a sporting event

players
contestants
participants
adversary
opposition
substitute
defender
spectators
programme
arena
stadium
pavilion
umpire
referee
decision
début
racket
innings
volley
gymkhana
climax
highlight
stamina
strategy

international
amateur
professional
spectacular
sensational
accurate
absorbing
aggressive
competitive
official
resourceful
successful
menacing
strenuous
anxious
graceful
polished
agile
dexterous
athletic
superhuman
dynamic
superb
resounding

concentrate
outwit
overwhelm
challenge
exhort
encourage
retaliate
react
participate
encroach
retrieve
reproach
congratulate
dismiss
sprawl
defeat
redeem
retire
penalize
practise
exhaust
massage
represent
sponsor

Phrases

held spellbound
against the clock
a successful partnership
roar of approval

a subdued silence
an Olympic hope
a masterly performance
the turning point

1	2	3
suspend	temperate	treasure
suspense	vibrate	pleasure
suspension	accurate	adventure
dispense	accurately	signature
incense	deliberate	sculpture

4	5	6
confusion	physics	scent
profusion	critic	ascent
infusion	critical	crescent
allusion	artistic	crescendo
illusion	realistic	descent

7	8	9
demolish	success	surveyor
flourish	access	dormitory
radish	accession	remorse
establish	account	rhetoric
establishment	accompany	oracle

10	11	12
*transcribe	*transcription	**specimen
prescribe	prescription	prospect
describe	description	respect
manuscript	subscription	respectable
postscript	subscriber	spectacle

* Latin root *scribo* = I write
** Latin root *specio* = I look

Raising funds for charity

benefactor
contributor
sponsor
cause
gratitude
contribution
donation
cheque
undertaking
scheme
project
venue
permission
marshals
programme
activities
representative
advertisement
tombola
lottery
bric-à-brac
research
expectation
presentation

generous
benevolent
zealous
charitable
fruitful
indispensable
hilarious
humorous
enjoyable
suitable
imaginative
lucrative
profitable
determined
competent
arduous
unbeatable
challenging
ambitious
worthy
urgent
needy
neglected
under-privileged

collect
donate
contribute
receive
accept
amass
raffle
organize
improvise
supervise
assist
persuade
enlist
volunteer
compliment
achieve
auction
canvass
participate
surpass
calculate
publicize
alleviate
allocate

Phrases

a worthwhile cause
unstinting support
successful venture
an urge to help

overwhelming generosity
fashion show
free publicity
"sponsored walk"

1	2	3
queue	reliable	motion
quote	arable	emotion
quotation	suitable	devotion
quench	peaceable	promotion
quarantine	changeable	locomotion

4	5	6
occupy	dangerous	spacious
justify	ruinous	vicious
modify	covetous	suspicious
qualify	ravenous	delicious
satisfy	dexterous	malicious

7	8	9
agitate	prairies	sensitive
irritate	colonel	repetitive
imitate	lieutenant	transitive
dissipate	sleight (of hand)	fugitive
gravitate	recipe	lucrative

10	11	12
*spectator	**connect	**connection
prospector	construct	construction
inspector	conspire	constructor
doctor	convene	conspirator
instructor	conversation	conspiracy

* Suffix -or, -er = a person who
** Latin prefix con- = together, with

A day in the life of a policeman

crime
criminal
burglar
offence
investigation
surveillance
suspicion
evidence
clue
trial
magistrate
officer
sergeant
superintendent
detective
witness
accident
vigilance
identification
computer
cadet
emergency
inquiry
vicinity

observant
honest
incorruptible
worthwhile
responsible
demanding
interesting
stimulating
hazardous
dangerous
persistent
habitual
routine
painstaking
accurate
notorious
infamous
fatal
wicked
unreliable
patient
tolerant
varied
resolute

interrogate
cross-examine
question
interview
escort
apprehend
arrest
detain
trace
search
discover
unearth
report
radio
caution
accuse
reprimand
patrol
record
consult
solve
direct
pursue
brief

Phrases

identity parade
lost property
disorderly conduct
missing persons

a bomb scare
an escaped prisoner
a motorway pile-up
a prime suspect

1	2	3
paralyse	violent	density
parasite	reverent	intensity
paragraph	adjacent	adversity
parachute	evident	necessity
paramount	eminent	reality

4	5	6
prohibit	duration	application
prohibitive	reputation	applicant
solicit	expectation	brilliant
solicitor	explanation	pittance
literature	calculation	sufferance

7	8	9
apparent	crystal	testament
apparel	cynic	amazement
appal	cylinder	arrangement
apparatus	pyramid	elementary
apparition	gymnast	supplementary

10	11	12
*confer	**subscribe	**submarine
conference	subdue	subway
reference	subject	substitute
referee	submerge	subsequent
difference	subnormal	subside

* Latin root *fero* = I bring, I bear
** Latin prefix *sub-* = below, under

A walking or cycling holiday

adventure
journey
excursion
expedition
tourist
companion
route
thoroughfares
byway
countryside
destination
vehicle
traveller
puncture
rucksack
provisions
village
hamlet
glade
plantation
foliage
facilities

incline
spanner

stationary
comfortable
wearisome
unsettled
fitful
tranquil
soggy
friendly
grateful
indebted
alternative
approximate
severe
arduous
ravenous
exhausted
miserable
reluctant
exhilarating

estimate
enquire
request
hail
encounter
indicate
direct
guide
meander
traverse
negotiate
retrace
overtake
dismantle
repair
inflate
connect
disconnect
consult
appreciate
explore
alight

Phrases

surrounding scenery
Ordnance Survey map
youth hostels
transport café
service station
overnight halt

inexpensive accommodation
weary and footsore
sun-drenched landscape
off the beaten track
a secluded campsite
a daunting prospect

1	2	3
chaos	pension	saucer
chord	tension	saucy
Christ	television	slaughter
echo	decision	fraud
stomach	precision	defraud

4	5	6
solve	ski	assistant
solvent	sketch	descendant
solution	skeleton	buoyant
resolve	skewer	sergeant
resolution	skirmish	peasant

7	8	9
student	route	skill
torment	routine	skilfully
parchment	around	wilfully
enjoyment	surround	fulfil
accompaniment	boundary	fulfilled

10	11	12
*conclusion	**immune	**improper
exclude	immodest	impatient
include	impede	impossible
preclude	impediment	improbable
recluse	imperceptible	immature

* Latin root *claudo* = I shut
** Latin prefix *im-* = not

The day I was accused of shoplifting

gift token
store
supermarket
detective
manager
assistant
office
explanation
merchandise
display
receipt
cashier
customer
article
jewellery
camera
cassette
exit
entrance
elevator
counter
parcel
bargain

busy
crowded
jostling
laden
fumbling
modern
enormous
spacious
attractive
eye-catching
expensive
exquisite
casual
excited
frightened
innocent
wrongful
mistaken
suspicious
zealous
precipitous
awkward
embarrassing

wrap
examine
explain
mistake
confuse
resemble
invite
accompany
demonstrate
purchase
confirm
corroborate
deny
mortify
worry
annoy
believe
relieve
identify

inadvertently
indignantly
impatiently

Phrases

protesting vehemently
error in judgment
apologize profusely
fortunate encounter
restricted view

a simple explanation
accusing looks
complete misunderstanding
a salutary lesson
righteous indignation

Words with similar meaning

1	2	3
burn	cool	chatter
scorch	chilly	babble
singe	nippy	gabble
char	wintry	prattle

4	5	6
charm	title	fair
delight	heading	festival
bewitch	headline	fête
captivate	caption	carnival

7	8	9
job	cross	abrupt
occupation	irritable	gruff
profession	quarrelsome	rude
business	cantankerous	brusque

10	11	12
quarrel	rub	sure
brawl	polish	positive
fracas	buff	certain
riot	burnish	definite

Concise descriptions

Compositions which require exact information about common objects or actions need careful thought. Often the writer omits certain details and as a result the description is not sufficiently exact.

You must remember two very important rules for compositions which ask you to describe certain things or actions:
1. Give a detailed rather than a general description.
2. Make sure that the sequence of ideas is correct. That means arranging the details in a definite order and avoiding setting them down in a haphazard manner.

Write a paragraph describing each of the following:
1. a vacuum flask
2. purchasing a postal order
3. sending a parcel by post
4. using a record player
5. exchanging a library book
6. planting a packet of seeds
7. taking a photograph
8. sewing on a button
9. making a pot of tea
10. a pocket torch
11. cleaning your teeth
12. making a bed

Recipes

In writing a recipe you should list the ingredients and then describe, in correct sequence, each step in preparing the dish.

Write a recipe for preparing the following:
1. boiled potatoes
2. chocolate crispies
3. bacon and egg
4. your favourite dish

Words with similar meaning

1

advise
counsel
suggest
recommend

2

warm
friendly
sociable
affable

3

abandon
desert
evacuate
surrender

4

annoy
irritate
infuriate
aggravate
tease

5

worried
anxious
concerned
perturbed
tense

6

surprised
bewildered
astounded
flabbergasted
bemused

7

story
tale
anecdote
narrative
account

8

cruel
wicked
brutal
ruthless
merciless

9

crooked
twisted
askew
awry
squint

10

clumsy
ungainly
awkward
cumbersome
hulking

11

sharp
acute
astute
shrewd
sagacious

12

flaw
fault
blemish
defect
imperfection

Mood

In some writing, mood plays a major part in making your reader feel that he is involved.

Here is a suggested outline for writing this kind of composition:

1. Set the scene. Describe how, where and when the event happened.
2. Capture the right mood by selecting important details which highlight the atmosphere.
3. Convey your feelings through careful choice of words and phrases.

Here are some things for you to describe. Try to form a picture in your own mind and convey this and the correct mood to your reader. Remember you can present your work in different ways, for example, as a story, a poem or a letter.

1. A dead bird
2. A city street at night
3. A caged lion
4. The dawn chorus
5. A crowded train
6. An unemployed person
7. A gold medal winner at the Olympic Games
8. A large store during a sale
9. A hospital ward
10. A circus elephant
11. A road accident
12. A wedding
13. A forest fire
14. A dustman clearing up rubbish after a football match

Words with similar meaning

1

weak
feeble
frail
infirm
decrepit

2

slender
slim
lean
gaunt
emaciated

3

push
shove
jostle
nudge
knock

4

trip
outing
expedition
jaunt
excursion

5

mourn
sorrow
grieve
lament
bewail

6

curious
prying
meddlesome
inquisitive
nosey

7

question
cross-examine
quiz
interrogate

8

offensive
disagreeable
abhorrent
detestable

9

stupid
dense
ignorant
obtuse

10

notable
famous
renowned
celebrated
distinguished

11

disgraceful
infamous
wicked
dastardly
evil

12

dim
faint
vague
obscure
indistinct

The season I like best

Suggested outline

1. **Introduction**
   The four seasons of the year—each possesses its own special charm

2. **Body of essay**

   (Take the four seasons in turn and describe the beauties, etc., connected with each.)

   a Spring—dawn of new life in hedgerow and fields—trees, birds, animals
   b Summer—nature matures—charm of meadow and mountain, stream and shrubland—lengthening days
   c Autumn—golden harvests—autumn tints—mists
   d Winter—nature slumbers—snow and ice—darkness

3. **Conclusion**
   Sum up—indicate which season you prefer, giving specific reasons for your choice—decision governed by personal taste and whether living in town or country

Here are other topics you could write about in the same way.

My favourite colour
The musical instrument I like best
The type of book I like best

Words with similar meaning

1

ill-mannered
pert
impudent
insolent
impertinent

2

unusual
queer
incredible
bizarre
strange

3

argue
dispute
debate
wrangle
quarrel

4

wonderful
miraculous
magnificent
superb

5

mean
miserly
stingy
niggardly

6

frown
scowl
glare
glower

7

keepsake
memento
relic
souvenir

8

pretend
impersonate
masquerade
pose

9

old-fashioned
outmoded
antiquated
obsolete

10

lovely
delightful
charming
fetching
beautiful

11

loyal
dependable
steadfast
staunch
reliable

12

unhappy
mournful
depressed
downcast
dejected

Road safety

Suggested outline

1. **Introduction**
   Increase in volume and speed of modern traffic—results
2. **Cause of road accidents**
   a Thoughtlessness of pedestrians
   b Highways—narrow, congested dangerous bends and corners, road surfaces—reconstruction for modern needs
   c Speed of travel
   d Reckless driving—human element—fatigue of drivers
3. **Plans to reduce accidents**
   Speed-limit in built-up areas—traffic lights—pedestrian crossings—school signs—police and road patrols—motorways
4. **Rules to be observed**
   Highway Code—rules for pedestrians, cyclists and motorists
5. **Summing up**
   Heavy toll of road accidents to be reduced—further helpful suggestions

Here are other topics you could write about in the same way:
   Safety in the home
   Pollution
   Conservation

Words with similar meaning

1

headstrong
stubborn
wilful
obstinate
tenacious

2

proud
vain
arrogant
haughty
conceited

3

stay
dwell
occupy
inhabit
reside

4

blame
accuse
charge
indict

5

grief
distress
sorrow
anguish

6

prevent
avoid
avert
forestall

7

friend
companion
playmate
acquaintance

8

gather
meet
assemble
convene

9

surprise
astonish
amaze
astound

10

burden
handicap
disadvantage
hindrance
impediment

11

fury
wrath
rage
frenzy
passion

12

disturbance
rumpus
commotion
tumult
uproar

My favourite hobby

Suggested outline

1. **Introduction**
   What is a hobby? —pleasure derived from interest in a hobby

2. **Various hobbies**
   Stamp-collecting, drama, cycling and hiking, photography, painting, keeping pets, gardening, bird-watching, plane-spotting, neddlework, playing a musical instrument, dancing

3. **The favourite**
   Why selected by you as your chosen pursuit distinct from your regular routine of daily studies at school —detailed description of the hobby; indicate how it maintains interest all the year round

4. **Summing up**
   General review of hobbies —then value, especially in connection with the increase in hours of leisure

Here are other topics you could write about in a similar way:

   The holiday I would like best
   My choice of career
   If I had three wishes

Words with similar meaning

1

tired
lifeless
drowsy
listless
lethargic

2

offend
embarrass
mortify
affront
humiliate

3

lined
furrowed
wrinkled
wizened
haggard

4

scatter
dispel
disperse
dissipate

5

boring
humdrum
tedious
monotonous

6

beat
time
tempo
rhythm

7

increase
enlarge
extend
expand

8

let
hire
rent
lease

9

real
natural
authentic
genuine

10

skilful
proficient
adept
expert
deft

11

immense
huge
gigantic
enormous
colossal

12

sad
dispirited
dejected
sorrowful
downhearted

Discussion

When writing this kind of composition you have to take into account opposing viewpoints on the subject.

Here is a suggested outline for writing this kind of composition:
1. State your opinion
2. Give evidence to support your opinion
3. Put the case for a different viewpoint
4. Show how your argument is stronger

Here are some topics for you to discuss:
  School uniform should be compulsory
  Corporal punishment should have been abolished
  Boys and girls should attend the same school
  Animals should not be used in circuses
  School years are the best of your life
  Smoking should be outlawed
  Blood sport is uncivilized
  There is a need for capital punishment
  All boys should be taught cookery at school
  Advertising is necessary
  Britain needs a Channel tunnel
  The school leaving age should be lowered
  It is better to be a participant in sport than a spectator
  Factory farming is cruel

Words with similar meaning

1	2	3
foretell	old	intrigue
predict	aged	fascinate
prophesy	elderly	enchant
forecast	ancient	captivate
foresee	antique	interest

4	5	6
shortage	dislike	plain
scarcity	loathe	clear
dearth	abhor	obvious
deficiency	detest	evident

7	8	9
crush	joy	wander
crease	delight	stroll
wrinkle	rapture	saunter
crumple	ecstasy	ramble

10	11	12
poor	shorten	watch
down-and-out	condense	view
penniless	summarize	observe
destitute	abbreviate	regard
impecunious	abridge	survey

Personal letters

25 High Street,
Newtown,
West County, AB1 2CD
1st June, 1981

Dear Mary,

Thank you for the book you lent me. I agree it was the funniest in the series.

Have you made any further holiday plans yet? I hope to go camping in the Lake District in the first week in August. Does this appeal to you? If so, we can discuss it next week at the disco.

Yours sincerely,

Susan

1. Remember every letter requires:
   - *a*   your address
   - *b*   the date
   - *c*   the greeting
   - *d*   the ending
   - *e*   your signature
2. Write a letter to a friend
   - *a*   thanking him/her for a birthday gift;
   - *b*   inviting him/her to spend a weekend with you;
   - *c*   congratulating him/her on winning a prize of £50 in a competition.
3. Write a letter to your parent(s) describing an enjoyable party you have attended while on holiday.
4. Recently you wrote a letter to your friend telling him/her you would shortly be leaving school. Write your friend's reply.

Words with similar meaning

1

urge
coax
persuade
entice
exhort

2

stout
plump
rotund
corpulent
robust

3

event
incident
occurrence
happening
spectacle

4

jump
spring
leap
bound

5

show
display
demonstrate
exhibit

6

state
declare
assert
certify

7

brave
gallant
heroic
courageous

8

singular
extraordinary
unusual
unique

9

spotted
speckled
mottled
flecked

10

promptly
immediately
instantly
directly
forthwith

11

impressive
imposing
stately
majestic
prepossessing

12

annoying
troublesome
aggravating
irksome
irritating

Addressing envelopes

The Managing Director
Smith and Son Ltd
Anytown
Anywhere E54 5FG

Forms of address

To individuals:
>Master S. Smith
>Mr S. Smith
>S. Smith Esq.
>Rev. S. Smith
>Prof. S. Smith
>Dr S. Smith or S. Smith Esq., M.D.
>The Very Rev. the Dean of . . .

To firms:
>Messrs J. Payne & Co.
>The Metropolitan Gas Board
>The S.R.Q.R. Tea Co. Stores

But note the following:
>Roberts and Son Ltd
>X.Y. Zebra & Co., Ltd

Address an envelope:
1.   to yourself;
2.   to the Head Teacher of your school;
3.   to one of your friends.

Words with similar meaning

1	2	3
soft	broken	savage
feathery	irregular	brutal
furry	fitful	fierce
fluffy	sporadic	vicious
downy	interrupted	ferocious

4	5	6
weak	sulk	vivid
delicate	fret	striking
fragile	grumble	dazzling
flimsy	complain	brilliant

7	8	9
perfumed	rough	threadbare
scented	crude	shabby
fragrant	coarse	worn
aromatic	uncouth	seedy

10	11	12
admire	lazy	source
value	indolent	beginning
respect	idle	origin
esteem	slothful	derivation

Conversations

"Come on, you'll be late for school," the mother chided her son.

"Shan't," came the faint reply from the bedroom.

"Why, what's wrong?" the mother enquired.

"The teachers hate me and the kids despise me," said the son with a sob in his voice.

"I'll give you two good reasons why you should go," the mother chided.

"What are they?" the son asked querulously.

"One—you're forty-one," said the mother firmly, "and two—you're the headmaster."

(adapted from the "Puffin Crack-a-Joke Book")

When writing conversations the following points have to be observed:

1. Have a general idea of the course of the conversation, i.e. what climax will be reached.
2. Let each remark arise out of the preceding one.
3. Indicate the actual words spoken by each speaker by inserting quotation marks in their correct positions.

Words which can be used instead of "said":

added	interposed	murmured	replied
interrupted	continued	observed	shouted
retorted	exclaimed	remarked	whispered

Write a conversation between:

1. two boys returning home after watching a football match—each boy supports a different team;
2. Mrs A and Mrs B upon a recent happening in your town or village;
3. Mr Grumble and Mr Cheery.

Words with similar meaning

1

murder
assassinate
slaughter
massacre
decimate

2

conduct
manners
behaviour
deportment
demeanour

3

howl
bawl
yell
screech
scream

4

enemy
foe
adversary
opponent

5

piece
fragment
particle
morsel

6

suggest
hint
imply
infer

7

rash
hasty
impulsive
impetuous

8

lively
alert
vivacious
wide-awake

9

valuable
invaluable
precious
priceless

10

unfriendly
hostile
militant
belligerent

11

goods
cargo
shipment
freight

12

dismiss
discharge
acquit
release

Writing a play

For play-writing you should:

1. Study carefully the lay-out of a play. You may find one in your school reader or in a book of plays borrowed from the library.
2. Decide the type of play you intend to write — whether it is to be a fairy-tale, comedy, tragedy, etc.
3. Think of the plot — a play must have a beginning, a middle or turning point, and an ending. These should follow in natural sequence.
4. Plan out your scenes.
5. Write the dialogue for each character. Try to make the characters sound as real as you can.
6. Revise the plot and the dialogue, introducing a little more here and cutting out a little there. Your main object is to interest an audience and to secure "action" throughout.
7. Lastly, invent a suitable title for the play and insert any stage directions.

Write a short play suitable for a group of young children to act. Here are some suggestions for subjects you could use:

1. A favourite fairy story, e.g. "Snow-White and the Seven Dwarfs", or "Goldilocks and the Three Bears"
2. A group of pupils who set out to investigate the disappearance of the School Sports' Trophy
3. A play which has a background of some historical event connected with your locality

Business letters

41 Low Avenue,
Merryton,
Wellshire, WX7 8YZ

1st June, 1981

The Manager,
Seasoned Timbers, Ltd.,
Wood Lane,
Anytown, PQ5 6ST

Dear Sir,
    Please send me a catalogue of your garden sheds as advertised in "The Chronicle", on Saturday, 4th May, 1981.

Yours faithfully,

Thomas Cook

Remember business letters require:
1. your address
2. the date
3. the name and address of the person to whom you are writing
4. the greeting (which is formal)
5. the ending (which is formal)
6. your signature (including your surname)

Your letter should be *brief, courteous* and to the point.

Here are some business letters for you to write. Make up suitable names and addresses.

1. Write a letter to a plumber requesting an estimate for the cost of replacing the washhand basin in your bathroom.

2. Write to a firm which has advertised camping holidays on the Continent asking them to send you their holiday brochure for next season.

3. Write to a bookseller asking him to send you a copy of a book.

4. Write to a hotel to make a reservation for a week's holiday you intend to spend in Scarborough.
   Write the manager's reply.

5. Answer this advertisement:
   Pye stereo record player in excellent condition. Cost £90. Best offer secures. Apply in writing to Box 41, "Evening Post", Nile Court, Newtown.

6. Write a letter to a firm informing them of the non-arrival of certain goods you ordered.
   Write the firm's reply.

7. Write a letter to a newspaper complaining about the fact that owners of dogs are allowing them to foul the pavements of your town or village.

8. Write to a firm from whom you bought a new raincoat, complaining that after wearing the garment once, the lining seams came apart.

Posters

You must have noticed posters or placards in public places advertising meetings and entertainments. Such posters come from the printer or sign-writer and are often posted by a person called a bill-poster.

However, you can make your own posters, thus providing excellent training in printing, colouring and arrangement. When preparing a poster the following points have to be borne in mind:
1. Make the most important facts "stand out", i.e. use larger and heavier lettering.
2. Give *all* the necessary details, such as the day, the time, the place, prices of admission, etc.
3. Never overcrowd the poster, i.e. use as few words as possible.

Examine the poster opposite carefully. Does it contain all the necessary details? Could you improve on the design? How?

Here are some posters for you to prepare:
1. Advertise a concert to be given by pupils of your school.
2. Draw up a poster advertising a "final" football or netball match in which your school team is to take part.
3. Draw up a poster announcing some event in connection with your local Scout or Guide Troop.
4. Design a poster advertising a Jumble Sale.
5. Draw up a poster announcing that there will be an end-of-term school dance.

PANTOMIME
CINDERELLA

Presented By
THE PUPILS OF TREETOP SCHOOL

in the

S C H O O L   H A L L,
P L Y M S T O L

MONDAY, 23RD DECEMBER

Doors open 7.00 p.m. Commences 7.30 p.m.

SEATS ... £1.00 AND 75p
(children under 14 yrs 50p)

PROCEEDS IN AID OF SAVE THE CHILDREN FUND

Roots, prefixes, suffixes

What is the meaning of the part in bold type in each of the following words?

Round 1

ex**port**
export
export**er**
connect

re-echo
mariner
primrose
transplant

de**scribe**
describe
mov**able**
ref**ere**nce

Round 2

post**script**
postscript
depressed
glazi**er**

precaution
hope**ful**
thorn**y**
immature

ex**clude**
exclude
flex**ible**
recline

Round 3

congregate
beauti**ful**
interpose
preface

re**port**
report
report**er**
en**clo**sure

trans**port**
transport
impossible
degrade

Round 4

trans**fer**
transfer
transfer**able**
pre**dict**

in**spect**
inspect**or**
mermaid
manu**script**

re**serve**
reserve
milk**y**
ed**ible**

Round 5

spectator
spect**ator**
recall
in**clude**

portable
port**able**
premier
postdate

impious
construct
construct**or**
interfere

52

Difficult words

1

fulfil
fulfilment
fulfilled
fulfilling

2

handicap
handicapped
kidnap
kidnapped

3

omit
omitted
quarrel
quarrelled

4

misprint
misfortune
mischief
mistake

5

pronounce
pronunciation
renounce
renunciation

6

specimen
independence
misdemeanour
behaviour

7

panic
panicky
mimic
mimicked

8

picnic
picnicked
benefit
benefited

9

all right
stationary (at rest)
stationery
encyclopaedia

10

forcible
negligible
gullible
collapsible

11

conscience
conscientious
science
conscious

12

humour
humorous
isosceles
octahedron

Difficult words

1

rhythm
arctic
embarrass
excellent

2

cancel
cancelled
commit
committed

3

lantern
good-bye
courteous
journey

4

commencement
knowledgeable
management
manageable

5

parallel
parallelogram
prefer
preferred

6

ice
icy
pebble
pebbly

7

programme
envelope
forehead
forecast

8

connection
complexion
persuade
exert

9

guerrilla
irresistible
foresee
forefinger

10

accommodation
separate
sheriff
calendar

11

argument
forgivable
sizeable
movable

12

mantelpiece
neighbour
manoeuvre
briquette

Difficult words

1

sergeant
colonel
corporal
lieutenant

2

sincerely
kilometre
pursue
posthumous

3

legible
illegible
responsible
irresponsible

4

restaurant
bereavement
souvenir
councillor

5

acquaintance
indispensable
probable
changeable

6

paraffin
lightning
preventive
somersault

7

suspicious
successful
woollen
bulletin

8

inveigle
connoisseur
definitely
amateur

9

noticeable
considerable
agreeable
fashionable

10

immediately
fascinate
artificial
precision

11

radiator
refrigerator
automaton
foreign

12

suppress
mattress
assassinate
reminiscence

Do you know where these sayings came from?

Crocodile tears —false sorrow

A dog in the manger —a person who will neither use something nor allow others to do so

To show the white feather —to show cowardice

Swan song —final act or deed

To cut the Gordian Knot —to overcome a difficulty in one step

Sword of Damocles —threat of impending disaster

A skeleton in the cupboard —a family secret

To work the oracle —to persuade someone to adopt your ideas by subterfuge

The lion's share —all or nearly all

To get into hot water —to get into trouble

Flogging a dead horse —persisting in doing something when there is obviously no hope of success

To wear one's heart upon one's sleeve —to make one's feelings obvious

Like greased lightning —very fast indeed

To go against the grain —to go against one's inclination or contrary to the norm

To rise like a Phoenix from the ashes —to come to life again

To foot the bill —to pay the account

He who pays the piper calls the tune —a person who finances a venture can dictate the policy

Forlorn hope —an impossible dream

Devil's advocate —someone who takes the opposite side for the sake of causing an argument

Taboo —something that is forbidden

A bolt from the blue —a sudden and unexpected happening

Blackmail —payment extorted by intimidation

To ring true —to sound genuine

To let the cat out of the bag —to disclose a secret

Hoist with your own petard —caught in your own trap

Job's comforter —a person who tries to comfort you but by saying the wrong thing makes things worse

To give no quarter —to be inflexible or to give no mercy

A Philistine —an ignorant person

A vandal —a person who wilfully destroys something

To run with the hare and hunt with the hounds — to play a double and deceitful game, to be a traitor

A Trojan horse —a hidden danger

To kill the fatted calf —to celebrate with the best of everything

To throw down the gauntlet —to challenge

An Amazon —a strong woman

To pass the Rubicon —to take an irrevocable step (one from which there is no return)

To meet one's Waterloo —to meet with defeat

One's Achilles' heel —a vulnerable or weak spot

In the Doldrums —to be depressed

If the mountain will not come to Mohammed, Mohammed must go to the mountain — if one person won't give in then the other must

Judas kiss —an active betrayal

Hobson's choice —no choice at all

To go by Shanks's pony —to go on foot

Red tape —tiresome rules and regulations

To be on tenterhooks —to be in impatient suspense

To nail your colours to the mast —to state uncompromisingly what you believe

Abbreviations

A.A.	—Automobile Association
A.B.A.	—Amateur Boxing Association
B.B.C.	—British Broadcasting Corporation
C	—Centigrade
C.I.D.	—Criminal Investigation Department
C.O.D.	—Cash on Delivery
D.H.S.S.	—Department of Health and Social Security
do	—Ditto (the same)
E.E.C.	—European Economic Community
F.A.	—Football Association
G.M.T.	—Greenwich Mean Time
i.e.	—id est (that is)
I.M.F.	—International Monetary Fund
I.T.A.	—Independent Television Authority
Ltd	—Limited
m.p.h.	—Miles per hour
NATO	—North Atlantic Treaty Organization
N.C.B.	—National Coal Board
O.H.M.S.	—On Her Majesty's Service
P.T.O.	—Please turn over
R.A.C.	—Royal Automobile Club
R.I.P.	—Requiescat in Pace (Rest in Peace)
R.S.P.C.A.	—Royal Society for the Prevention of Cruelty to Animals
R.S.V.P.	—Répondez s'il vous plaît (please reply)
T.U.C.	—Trades Union Congress
U.K.	—United Kingdom
UNESCO	—United Nations Economic, Social and Cultural Organization
V.I.P.	—Very Important Person
viz	—namely
Y.M.C.A.	—Young Men's Christian Association

About parliament (French *parler* = to speak)

Bill	—The draft of a proposed law
Act	—A bill which has become law after it has been presented in parliament three times
Sitting	—A parliamentary day
Session	—A year's sitting of parliament
Speaker	—The person who acts as chairman in the House of Commons
Dissolve	—To end a parliament. This is done by the King or Queen
Prorogue	—To discontinue the meeting of parliament, e.g. for holidays. Any bill which has not been presented three times has to be reintroduced after prorogation
Adjourn	—To discontinue business. After an adjournment business is resumed where it left off
Minister	—The head of a government department
Cabinet	—A small committee of ministers under the Prime Minister
Division	—The taking of a vote on a subject that has been discussed. This is done by Members of Parliament passing out of the House by different lobbies
House of Lords	—The upper house of the British parliament. The House of Lords can delay the passing of a bill for one year
Lord Chancellor	—The Speaker of the House of Lords. The Lord Chancellor is a chief judge and keeps the Great Seal of State used to authenticate new laws passed by parliament
Woolsack	—The seat of the Lord Chancellor

About cathedrals and churches

Chancel —The eastern part reserved for clergy and choir and usually railed off

Nave —The body of the church from the inner door to the chancel

Aisles —The north and south wings separated from the nave by pillars. The word aisle is also applied to the passage between rows of pews

Transept —Many cathedrals are cruciform (cross-shaped) in arrangement, and the north and south transepts are the arms of the transverse (crosswise) part

West Door —The principal doorway of a cathedral

Crypt —Underground cell or chapel

Cloister —A covered arcade usually joining a monastery with the church

Belfry —The bell tower

About the theatre

Theme —The subject or topic about which the play is written

Act —Part of a play, divided into scenes or performed straight on without the fall of the curtain

Scene —A continuous part of a play during which there is no change of place or time

Comedy —A dramatic production which is of a light and amusing nature and which may have a happy ending

Plot	—The story
Tragedy	—A production which raises pity or fear and usually has a sad ending
Melodrama	—An extravagantly tragic and unreal play
Mime	—Acting without words
Opera	—A dramatic production in which the actors sing their parts to the accompaniment of an orchestra instead of speaking them
Repertory Theatre	—A theatre with a company of actors and actresses regularly attached to it, different plays being performed every week
Producer	—The person who presents the play on stage
Director	—The person who manages the business involved in the production of a play
Playwright	—The person who writes the play
Ballet	—A dramatic story expressed on the stage by means of dancing
Choreography	—The composition and arrangement of dancing
Auditorium	—The part of a theatre reserved for the audience
Audition	—A trial performance given by an actor seeking a part in a dramatic production
Understudy	—A substitute ready to take an actor's part if he becomes ill

About meetings

Chairman —Chosen to preside over a meeting

Secretary —Conducts the correspondence and keeps the records

Agenda —List of matters to be discussed at a meeting

Minutes Book —The book in which the minutes (or summary of proceedings) of a meeting are recorded

Motion —A formal proposal put forward for the consideration of the meeting. A motion must be moved by one person and seconded by another before other members can discuss the proposal

Amendment —Words introduced into or deleted from a motion and which profess to improve the original motion

Proxy —Authorization to vote on behalf of someone in his absence

About shops

Retail Dealer —Sells to the general public

Wholesaler —Supplies the retailer

Net Weight —Actual weight of the goods

Gross Weight —Weight of the goods plus packaging

Receipt —A written acknowledgment of money received

VAT (Value Added Tax) —A tax on the increase in value of a product due to manufacturing and marketing

Hire Purchase —A system of buying goods by paying in instalments

Proverbs or sayings

Birds of a feather flock together
Cut your coat according to your cloth
Nothing venture nothing gain
There are none so deaf as those who will not hear
You can lead a horse to water but you can't make it drink
Absence makes the heart grow fonder
Discretion is the better part of valour
Necessity is the mother of invention
A drowning man will clutch at a straw
A fool and his money are soon parted
A rolling stone gathers no moss
Pride goes before a fall
A bird in the hand is worth two in the bush
Look before you leap
Empty vessels make most noise
Let sleeping dogs lie
Imitation is the sincerest form of flattery
As you make your bed so must you lie in it
Every cloud has a silver lining
Forbidden fruit tastes sweetest
One swallow does not make a summer
Faint heart never won fair lady
Great oaks from little acorns grow
The early bird catches the worm
Silence gives consent
He who hesitates is lost
A stitch in time saves nine
No news is good news
Don't count your chickens before they are hatched
A cat may look at a king
Still waters run deep
To err is human, to forgive divine

Unusual occupations

Courier —a travelling attendant
Curator —in charge of a museum or art gallery
Entomologist —studies insects
Farrier —shoes horses
Fletcher —makes arrows
Lapidary —cuts precious and semi-precious stones
Mason —cuts, prepares and lays stones used in building
Ornithologist —studies birds
Seismologist —studies earthquakes
Taxidermist —stuffs and mounts skins of animals

Occupations related to health

Bacteriologist —studies bacteria
Dietitian —specializes in planning food
Geriatrician —specializes in the care of old people
Haematologist —studies the blood
Paediatrician —specializes in children's diseases
Physiotherapist —treats by exercise and massage
Radiographer —takes X-ray photographs

Roman numerals

I	one	XI	eleven	XXX	thirty
II	two	XII	twelve	XL	forty
III	three	XIII	thirteen	L	fifty
IV	four	XIV	fourteen	LX	sixty
V	five	XV	fifteen	LXX	seventy
VI	six	XVI	sixteen	LXXX	eighty
VII	seven	XVII	seventeen	XC	ninety
VIII	eight	XVIII	eighteen	C	hundred
IX	nine	XIX	nineteen	D	five hundred
X	ten	XX	twenty	M	one thousand